Jim

Great presentation!

thank you for sharing
your expertise with us
this morning.

Jay Smyre
the Whitehall Club
3/15/2018

PORTRAIT OF
HOUSTON

PHOTOGRAPHY BY KATHY ADAMS CLARK
TEXT BY GARY CLARK

FARCOUNTRY
PRESS

FRONT COVER: Houston's modern skyline shines into view
from the pedestrian bridge over Buffalo Bayou.

BACK COVER: The historic Rice Hotel on Texas Avenue and
Main Street has been reborn as the Post Rice Lofts. In 1963,
President John F. Kennedy spent the night at the Rice Hotel
before traveling to Dallas where he was assassinated. Today
the building houses luxury apartments, restaurants, shops,
and meeting space.

FRONT FLAP, TOP: Reflected in the modern steel and glass
architecture of Memorial Hermann Hospital is the
traditional architecture of the Texas Medical Center.

FRONT FLAP, BOTTOM: Twilight view of Fred Hartman Bridge
spanning the Houston Ship Channel.

TITLE PAGE: The lights of a METRORail train streak past the
water features at Main Street Square in downtown Houston.

RIGHT: The downtown Houston skyline, as seen from
the Waugh Street overpass along the Allen Parkway.

ISBN 10: 1-56037-527-2
ISBN 13: 978-1-56037-527-2

© 2012 by Farcountry Press
Photography © 2012 by Kathy Adams Clark

For more information about our books, write Farcountry Press, P.O. Box 5630,
Helena, MT 59604; call (800) 821-3874; or visit www.farcountrypress.com.

Created, produced, and designed in the United States.
Printed in Korea.

17 16 15 14 13 12   1 2 3 4 5 6

FOREWORD

BY GARY CLARK

HOUSTON RESTS LIKE A GIANT HAND on the southeastern Texas coastal plain, with the palm and fingers of the city stretching over 8,778 square miles and hosting 5.9- million people (as recorded by the 2010 U.S. Census). The sixth-largest metropolitan area in the United States, Houston covers a landmass larger than the state of New Jersey. Hosting more than 2 million people within its city boundaries, Houston ranks fourth on the list of most populated U. S. cities following Chicago, Los Angeles, and New York City. Quite a feat for a town that in 1850 had only 2,396 inhabitants.

Within the fingers of Houston's outreached hand lie numerous micro-cities like Rice Village, University Park, and Missouri City. At the tips of its fingers and often within Houston's city limits or extraterritorial jurisdiction are master-planned and highly acclaimed suburban communities such as Clear Lake, Kingwood, and The Woodlands. The city's fingertips touch and facilitate the economies of many thriving outlying cities including Galveston, Baytown, Sugarland, Conroe, Katy, and Angleton.

Houston is home to forty colleges and universities including the Tier One–designated University of Houston, the world-renowned Rice University, plus the University of St. Thomas and Texas Southern University. Houston has also been a leader in the community college movement, with the Houston Community College System serving more than 75,000 students and the Lone Star College System, one of the state's largest community colleges, serving more than 75,000 students.

Not even brothers Augustus Chapman Allen and John Kirby Allen, who in August of 1836 founded Houston on the swampy, mosquito-infested banks of Buffalo Bayou, could have imagined the city that would emerge in the twenty-first century as a sprawling metropolis of modern skyscrapers, shopping malls, diverse culture, incomparable performing and visual arts, and, not the least of all, a business community as robust and bustling as any in the world. Houston's energy, aeronautics, and technology industries make it home to twenty-three Fortune 500 companies, ranking second only to New York City. Were Houston a nation unto itself, it would be the thirtieth-largest economy in the world. The dynamic city can boast of being the nation's nerve center for energy production; the home of NASA's Space Center that tracked the first landing of a man on the moon; a home for the world-class Houston Museum of Fine Arts; and a theater district concentrated in a seventeen-block downtown area that is surpassed only by the theater district of New York City. Houston's theater district includes the extraordinarily acclaimed Houston Symphony, Houston Grand Opera, and Houston Ballet, not to mention the Tony Award-winning Alley Theatre sitting only blocks from the original spot by the bayou where the Allen brothers founded Houston in the early nineteenth century.

Sports, like most other aspects of the city, are big in Houston. The quintessential Texas sport of football is famously spearheaded by the NFL Houston Texans playing at Reliant Stadium; America's pastime of baseball enlivens summer days with the MLB Houston Astros playing at Minute Maid Park; the fast-paced motion of basketball is nowhere better played than by the two-time world-champion NBA Houston Rockets playing at the Toyota Center; and the new enthusiasm for American soccer is being kicked forward by the Houston Dynamo Major League Soccer team playing at the BBVA Compass Stadium.

Green space for parks and outdoor recreation plays a vital role in Houston's

Beautiful statues complete with a fountain adorn the grounds of the Sugar Land City Hall.

lifestyle. The Trust for Public Land lists Houston's total green space at 56,405 acres, which makes the city first in park space among the nation's ten most-populous cities. The 1,431-acre Memorial Park, just west of downtown, is larger than New York City's Central Park. Buffalo Bayou flows thirty-five miles from the Katy Prairie area west of Houston through numerous city parks. Green space makes Houston a magnet for nature enthusiasts, who can enjoy an array of wildlife from deer to dragonflies, birds to butterflies. The city sits on the most important bird migratory route in North America, with billions of migratory birds passing between their winter homes in South America and summer nesting grounds in North America. In addition, many different species of migratory birds stop to nest in Houston.

Houston is not shy about its heritage as the onetime center for farming and ranching. Accordingly, the Houston Livestock Show and Rodeo, held every year between February and March, ranks among the largest in the world and attracts more than 2 million people. The rodeo event features twelve trail rides beginning several weeks before the event, with riders traveling on horseback from outlying areas, covering distances ranging from 70 to 386 miles.

Yet the modernization of Houston can be expressed no better than in its Texas Medical Center. As the world's largest medical center, it covers 21 million square feet with fourteen highly acclaimed hospitals, two trauma facilities, two specialty institutions, three prestigious medical schools, six nursing schools, and a school of dentistry. Its M. D. Anderson Hospital leads the world in cancer research.

Finally, Houston ranks as the most ethnically diverse city in the United States. More than ninety languages are routinely spoken on the streets of Houston. Cultural diversity makes the city seem like a giant United Nations headquarters, but with people working arm in arm to build an ever more vital, prosperous, and welcoming community.

ABOVE: Hermann Park, a 445-acre woodland park near the Texas Medical Center, features marigolds, salvia, and hamelia.

LEFT: The Preston Avenue Bridge crosses Buffalo Bayou at Sesquicentennial Park.

ABOVE: The folks at Mandola's Deli on Leeland Street have been serving casual Italian food since 1975. Joseph and Frank Mandola welcome guests to "come in for a meal, leave with a story."

LEFT: The elegant Gateway Fountain puts on a graceful show in front of the George R. Brown Convention Center.

ABOVE: The Museum of Cultural Arts Houston (MOCAH) installed these porcelain and glass tile mosaics, titled *Our History,* in front of Ryan Middle School to celebrate cultural diversity.

RIGHT: The Gerald D. Hines Waterwall Park stands on three acres near the Williams Tower in the Galleria. Eleven thousand gallons of water per minute spill over the sixty-four-foot, horseshoe-shaped wall.

ABOVE: Justin Yu and hundreds of other creative chefs are bringing contemporary cuisine to Houston.

LEFT: An aerial view of downtown, with the Toyota Center, home of the NBA's Houston Rockets and the AHL's Houston Aeros, in the lower right.

ABOVE: Smither Park on Munger Street is a project of the Orange Show Center for Visionary Art and artist Dan Phillips. The green park is built around a series of imaginative mosaics in memory of John H. Smither, former board member of the Orange Show and president of the Houston Ballet.

LEFT: *Tolerance,* one of seven sculptures in a downtown public art installation along Buffalo Bayou created by the Spanish sculptor Jaume Plensa. The sculptures are made of a stainless steel mesh consisting of letters from the Latin, Hebrew, Arabic, Chinese, Japanese, Korean, Greek, Hindi, and Cyrillic alphabets.

15

ABOVE, TOP AND BOTTOM: Classical architecture, with column detail (pictured above), at Lovett Hall on the Rice University campus.

LEFT: Lovett Hall houses Rice University's admissions offices and welcome center. Classes were first held at the university in 1912. The private school serves more than 6,000 students and is regarded as one of the best universities in the United States.

ABOVE: Japanese-style garden ornaments dot the tranquil grounds of the Japanese Garden in Hermann Park.

LEFT: The Japanese Garden is a cooperative venture between American and Japanese businesses that serves as a symbol of friendship between the two countries.

ABOVE: The San Jacinto Monument commemorates the battle for Texas independence that ended at this location in 1836 when the people of Texas, then called "Texians," defeated the Mexican Army under General Santa Anna and won independence from Mexico. A thirty-four foot star symbolizing the Lone Star Republic tops the 570-foot-tall monument.

RIGHT: Visitors can take an elevator 486 feet up to the observation floor of the San Jacinto Monument. On a clear day, the view includes the historic San Jacinto Battleground State Historic Site, Buffalo Bayou, and the busy Houston Ship Channel.

ABOVE: Artist Malou Flato created this vibrant mosaic scene on a bench in Market Square Park on Milam Street in downtown Houston.

LEFT: There's no mistaking Houston City Hall at night, with its bright LED lights.

ABOVE: The luxurious Hotel ZaZa sits on the edge of Hermann Park in the Museum District.

LEFT: The six-acre Houston Garden Center in Hermann Park is a popular venue for special events. The grounds contain rose and bulb gardens, in addition to other seasonal plantings.

RIGHT: A Houston Texans flag waves as a fan drives through town. The team has built an impressive record since joining the NFL in 2002.

FAR RIGHT: Reliant Stadium hosts Houston Texans games, the Houston Livestock Show and Rodeo, and many other popular events.

BELOW: In the Museum District, people frequently exercise and recreate along the paths that circle Rice University.

ABOVE: Photographers from a Leisure Learning Unlimited class hone their skills photographing the Gus S. Wortham Memorial Fountain on Allen Parkway.

FACING PAGE: Dedicated to the memory of Martin Luther King, Jr., Barnett Newman's *Broken Obelisk* rests in a reflecting pool outside the Rothko Chapel on the grounds of the Menil Collection.

THESE PAGES: Fresh local produce and flowers entice shoppers at the Urban Harvest Farmers Market in Houston.

ABOVE, TOP: The Mecom-Rockwell Colonnade and Fountain is located on the north end of Hermann Park on San Jacinto Street.

ABOVE, BOTTOM AND RIGHT: At the Museum of Fine Arts in the Museum District, classical and modern architecture stand side by side. The museum complex encompasses exhibit space, cafés, shopping, and gardens.

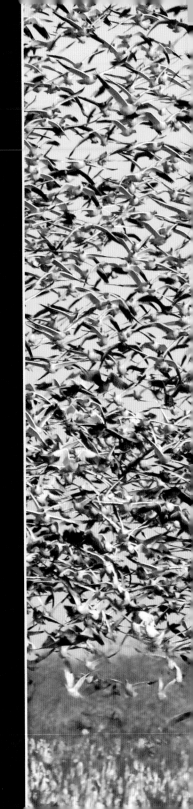

ABOVE, TOP AND BOTTOM: A lone kayaker and boaters take to the water at sunset.

ABOVE: Larger-than-life gargoyles greet visitors in Market Square Park downtown.

RIGHT: A dizzying view of downtown, including the circular skywalk over Smith Street.

ABOVE: Houston's sleek, modern METRORail runs from downtown to the Texas Medical Center. METRORail lines will one day crisscross the entire city.

LEFT: Minute Maid Park, on the eastern edge of downtown Houston, is home base for the Houston Astros baseball team.

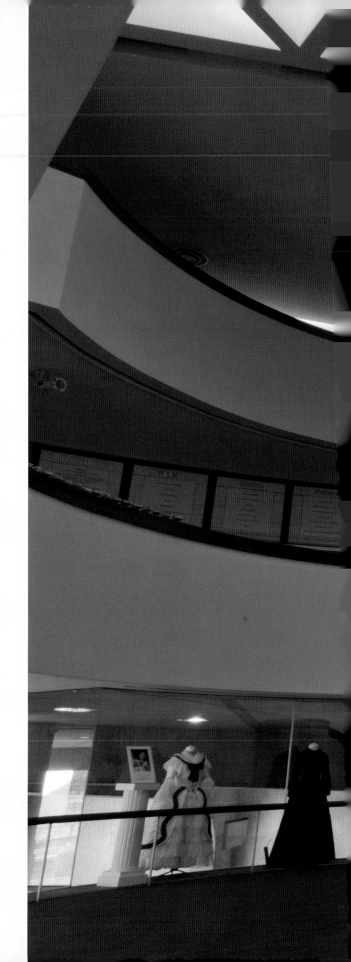

ABOVE, TOP: A Virtuosi of Houston Youth Orchestra harpist hones her skills. The organization's mission is to serve gifted young musicians by providing educational and performance opportunities.

ABOVE, BOTTOM: The Tony Award-winning Alley Theatre has been a fixture in Houston's cultural arts community for more than fifty years. Here a wig maker in the Alley's costume shop prepares for an upcoming production.

RIGHT: The stunning lobby of the Alley Theatre welcomes guests to the Hubbard Stage.

ABOVE: Cowboy boots are stylish as well as utilitarian at the Houston Livestock Show and Rodeo.

RIGHT: The carnival at the Livestock Show and Rodeo is enjoyed by people of all ages.

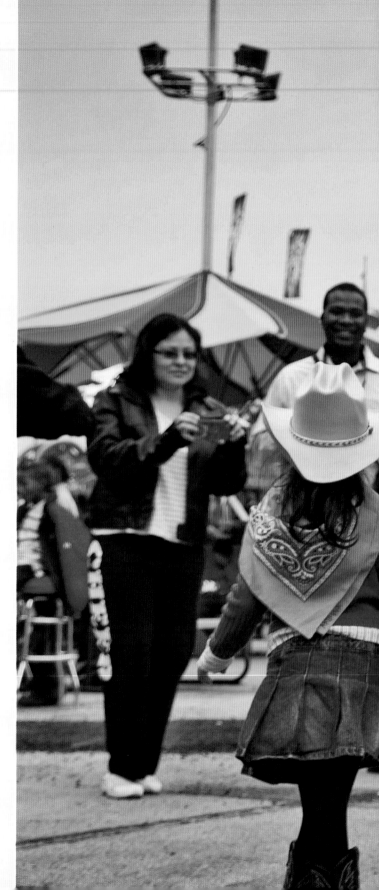

LEFT AND BELOW: The spectacular Fred Hartman Bridge spans the Houston Ship Channel between Baytown and La Porte. The largest cable-stayed bridge in Texas, it is named after the former editor and publisher of the *Baytown Sun* newspaper.

45

ABOVE: A sailboat glides along a residential lake in Houston.

LEFT: The Woodlands, a master-planned community north of
Houston, includes a world-class, open-air shopping district

ABOVE: A sign points the way to various attractions in Houston's exemplary Museum District.

LEFT: The Houston Museum of Natural Science in Hermann Park features a dynamic entrance plaza with a water feature and giant sundial.

ABOVE: Two parades are held each year to commemorate the life of Dr. Martin Luther King, Jr. Houston was the first city in the United States to honor Dr. King with a parade.

RIGHT: Waving in the breeze at the San Jacinto Battleground State Historic Site are, left to right, the U.S. flag, the Civil War-era Confederate flag, and the Texas state flag.

ABOVE: The Cockrell Butterfly Center at the Houston Museum of Natural Science houses free-flying butterflies plus exhibits and educational space.

FACING PAGE, TOP: A rice paper butterfly perches on a flower at the Cockrell Butterfly Center.

FACING PAGE, BOTTOM: Children ascend a flight of stairs to enter the forested habitat inside the Cockrell Butterfly Center.

ABOVE: The sculpture *Virtuoso* by David Adickes stands thirty-six feet tall outside the Lyric Building in Houston's Theater District.

RIGHT: The sculpture *A,A* by Jim Sanborn stands outside the M. D. Anderson Honors Library at the University of Houston. The metal sculpture contains phrases in English, Arabic, Russian, Chinese, and Spanish.

SANGRARAN LOS MURCIÉLAGOS
OCCASIONAL YOU THAT WHEN
NO WORD I SPOKE WAS EVER
WORLD OF SMILES AND LAUGHTER THAT
FEMINA QUID FACIAT, CUM SIT
T'ATTENDS. ALORS VIENS.
THE TABLECLOTH LIKE SOMETHING
DIFERENTES NO SON TAN DIFERENTES
ROMANCE ROMANCE SHOULD NEVER BEGIN
MAKVTES; "RET HVTHAKET ERA
STATUE OF ACHIL- LES. REALLY, THE THINGS
AGUA SOBRE LA PERMANENCIA Y EL
GARDER SON OMBRE. ELLE NE
STILL HAD A USE FOR THE HEART
ОТЧЕТЛИВО ВЫДЕЛЯЛИСЬ НА
OF BLINDER EYES AND ROLLS
LA TÊTE: CHARLES ÉTAIT LÀ.
ALMOST CHILDLIKE, AND MY
PROFUN- DAMENTE SUMIDA
ITS TOMB, DE- STROYED ITS RECORD
OUT OF POE. SHE TOUCHED
COMO LAS DOS MITADES DE
WITH SENTIMENT. IT SHOULD
THAT GO ON IN FRONT OF

ABOVE: Hubbell and Hudson is located on Waterway Avenue in The Woodlands shopping district, north of Houston. The store offers fresh breads, meats, seafood, fruits, and vegetables, plus a bistro, a bar, take-out service, and a cooking school.

LEFT: The Pumpkin House in Houston's historic Heights neighborhood is actually a modern building designed to match the early twentieth-century architecture of neighboring houses.

ABOVE, TOP: Many buildings in Houston's midtown and downtown areas have been renovated for urban dwelling, reinvigorating residential living in the center of Houston.

ABOVE, BOTTOM AND LEFT: The John P. McGovern Texas Medical Center Commons is a centrally located gathering place for the thousands of staff, patients, and visitors who come to the center daily.

ABOVE AND FACING PAGE, BOTTOM: The University of Houston–
Downtown is housed in the restored Merchants and Manufacturers
Building, with its cast-concrete Art Deco exterior.

FACING PAGE, TOP: Blooms of gulf muhly add color and texture
to area gardens and parks in the fall.

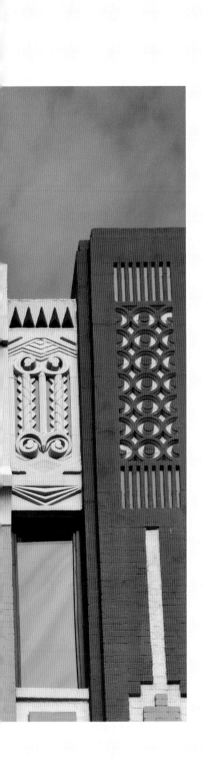

ABOVE, TOP: An anole lizard suns itself on a garden stump. These six- to eight-inch-long lizards are a common site around Houston neighborhoods.

ABOVE, BOTTOM: Wearing green and white, the AFC Veterans, part of the Alliance Futbol Club of the Houston Women's Soccer Association, take to the field at the Houston Amateur Sports Park.

LEFT: Project Row Houses is a program created by African American artists and activists in Houston's Third Ward. The houses include art spaces, artists' residences, and housing for young mothers.

ABOVE, TOP: American goldfinches are a common winter bird throughout the Houston area.

ABOVE, BOTTOM: Mosaic benches decorated with tiles by Malou Flato at Market Square Park on Milam Street provide an artful place to sit and enjoy the surroundings.

RIGHT: In addition to flower gardens and public art, Market Square Park features a dog run, a small Greek restaurant, and a memorial to Lauren Catuzzi Grandcolas, killed on United Flight 93 on September 11, 2001.

ABOVE: Resurrection Window, standing forty-feet tall and twenty-feet wide, graces the front of the Co-Cathedral of the Sacred Heart in downtown Houston.

RIGHT: A spectacular sunset silhouettes the Diving Bell Ferris Wheel at the Downtown Aquarium.

ABOVE: A redbud tree blooms in the spring at Jones County Park, north of Houston.

LEFT: The waters of Wortham Fountain in downtown Houston's Tranquility Park tumble down thirty-two levels. The park was dedicated in 1979 to celebrate the tenth anniversary of the Apollo 11 moon landing.

ABOVE: Businesses owned by people from China, Vietnam, and other Asian countries opened on the outskirts of downtown in the 1980s. Although many of the enterprises moved to the southwest part of town, some of the original colorful buildings still stand.

LEFT: Runners stream past endlessly in the 2012 half marathon portion of the Houston Marathon, established in 1972. The run ranks as the nation's premier winter marathon and also includes a 5K run and kids' fun run. Hosting more than 30,000 runners annually, the marathon is Houston's largest single-day sporting event.

THESE PAGES: The statue of General Sam Houston on horseback casts a shadow over the redbrick pathway and brilliant green lawns at Hermann Park. Unveiled in 1925, the statue stands above the circular drive at the north end of Hermann Park.

ABOVE: A black-and-white "tuxedo" cat soaks up some sun on the steps of a home in Houston's historic Heights neighborhood.

RIGHT: Situated in the Museum District, the Holocaust Museum Houston keeps the memory of the Holocaust alive and honors the survivors' legacy.

THESE PAGES: Signs direct visitors to the attractions at the Houston Zoo's African Forest exhibit, including chimpanzees and white rhinos.

Gus S. Wortham Theater Center

ABOVE: Situated in the city's Museum District, the Buffalo Soldier Museum preserves the legacy of African American soldiers since the founding of the first six all-African American units formed by Congress in 1866.

FACING PAGE: The Children's Museum, with 90,000 square feet of interactive exhibits, sits in the city's Museum District. Its colorful entrance is a sneak preview of the fun inside.

ABOVE: Mexican free-tailed bats emerge from under the Waugh Street Bridge where it crosses Buffalo Bayou just west of downtown Houston. The bat colony expands during the summer when female bats use the bridge as a nursery colony to raise their young.

LEFT: The International Space Station is a streak in the sky over The Woodlands, a suburban community north of Houston.

RIGHT: Billions of birds from the tropics migrate through the Upper Texas Coast each spring and fall. Many of them, like this hooded warbler, will stay to breed in the East Texas forests just north of Houston.

FAR RIGHT: A visitor enjoys a book in the shade of the Houston Audubon Society's Edith L. Moore Nature Sanctuary, west of downtown Houston.

BELOW: The Houston Arboretum in Memorial Park offers outdoor activities for adults and children plus a children's discovery center, classrooms for all ages, and demonstration gardens.

ABOVE: St. Paul's United Methodist Church was established in Houston in 1905, and its current home on Main and Binz streets dates back to 1930. The bells in the tower ring after each Sunday service and on special occasions.

ABOVE: The steeple of the Annunciation Catholic Church reaches into the sky above downtown Houston. The church was established in 1839, with the cornerstone of the current building laid in 1869.

FACING PAGE: The Heights neighborhood sits on a bluff four miles west of downtown and is lined with homes dating back to the early 1900s.

ABOVE, TOP: A visual communications class at Lone Star College–North Harris. Lone Star College System's six colleges spread from the northern part of Houston across northern Harris and southern Montgomery Counties. One of the largest community college systems in Texas, it enrolls more than 75,000 credit students.

ABOVE, BOTTOM: The *Houston Chronicle* is the seventh-largest daily newspaper in the country and the largest in Texas. Readers enjoy it in print, on the web, or on reading devices.

RIGHT: The Orange Show Center for Visionary Art began as a personal art project on Munger Street by Jeff McKissack. After his death, a nonprofit foundation was formed to preserve the project and support public art events in Houston.

ABOVE: *The Beer Can House* is a public art project managed by the Orange Show Center for Visionary Art. John Milkovisch began decorating his house in 1968 and eventually covered it entirely with whole or flattened beer cans. The house has become a Houston tourist attraction.

FACING PAGE: Downtown features energetic modern architecture.

ABOVE: Heritage Park in downtown Houston preserves buildings from the early days of the city's fledgling community.

LEFT: The Pierce Elevated, a part of Interstate 45, crosses over downtown Houston's surface streets and Buffalo Bayou.

ABOVE, TOP: Ruby-throated hummingbirds migrate through Houston by the tens of thousands during August and September on their way from the northern United States to the tropics, where they spend the winter.

ABOVE, BOTTOM: High-rise living affords stunning views of the city.

RIGHT: Cargo ships and tugboats move through the Houston Ship Channel. The Port of Houston ranks first in the nation for foreign waterborne tonnage shipped to the United States.

ABOVE, TOP: Runners, walkers, and bicyclists of all abilities enjoy the exercise trails that wind through Memorial Park.

ABOVE, BOTTOM: Dogs and their owners enjoy the green space along Buffalo Bayou in central Houston. Here a black labrador retriever plays his namesake game.

RIGHT: Sugar Land's Oyster Creek Park, on the west side of Houston, features a three-mile exercise loop, concert space, and picnic areas.

ABOVE: Texans love their bluebonnets. A maroon variety was developed by Texas A&M University to honor their school colors.

RIGHT: Canoeing is popular in early autumn on Lake Woodlands, north of the city.

THESE PAGES: Kemah Boardwalk, south of Houston alongside Galveston Bay, is an entertainment complex featuring amusement rides, dining, concerts, and hotel space.

ABOVE, TOP: Double-crested cormorants are among the most common birds along the coastal waterways and inland lakes around Houston.

ABOVE, BOTTOM: The Islamic Da'wah Center on Main Street in downtown Houston occupies the erstwhile Houston National Bank. The center offers prayer services and hosts special events.

LEFT: A study in form in the Houston skyline.

103

ABOVE: The statue of Gandhi in Hermann Park is the result of a cooperative effort between the City of Houston, the India Culture Center, and the Indian government. Dedicated in 2004, the statue stands on a grassy area near the Houston Garden.

LEFT: The Menil Collection constitutes the art collection of John and Dominique de Menil and forms a "Neighborhood of Art" with green space, outdoor art, and gallery space.

105

ABOVE, TOP AND BOTTOM: Children enjoy a playground in the Hilshire Village subdivision in Spring Branch, west of downtown Houston.

RIGHT: A full-sized Saturn V rocket and capsule used during the Apollo program is displayed at Rocket Park in the Johnson Space Center in Clear Lake, south of downtown Houston.

ABOVE: Vinca flowers in a suburban garden.

RIGHT: A gray hairstreak butterfly perches on a purple coneflower at the world-renowned Mercer Arboretum and Botanic Gardens along Spring Creek, north of Houston.

LEFT: A woman enjoys a walk in the woods along the Spring Creek Greenway Project in northern Harris County, on the northern perimeter of Houston.

ABOVE: Holiday decorations light up the night around City Hall and the Reflecting Pond in downtown Houston.

FACING PAGE: One of the many stunning water features at the Gus S. Wortham Memorial Fountain, designed by architect William Cannady in 1978.

ABOVE: The Williams Tower looms tall at twilight in the Galleria with its spotlight beaming to the heavens from the tower top.

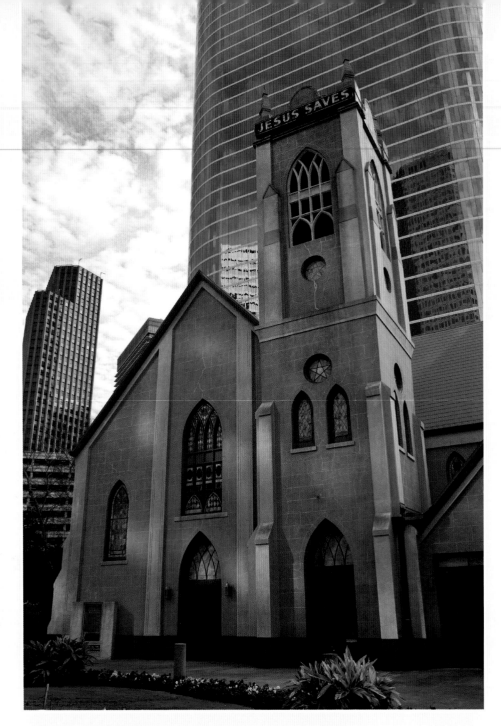

ABOVE: The Antioch Missionary Baptist Church is dwarfed by modern skyscrapers in downtown Houston. The church was originally built in 1875 and was remodeled to its current design in 1936.

RIGHT: The Harris County Courthouse in downtown Houston was built in 1910. A $65 million construction project in 2010 restored the building to its original design.

ABOVE, TOP AND LEFT: A celebration of life at the Cancer Survivors Plaza in Houston's Museum District. The statues are the work of Victor Salmones and show life-sized figures passing through a maze that symbolizes cancer treatment. The R. A. Bloch Cancer Foundation established the park in Houston.

ABOVE, BOTTOM: A wide variety of bicycling trails throughout Houston and surrounding suburbs make exercising fun and readily available.

115

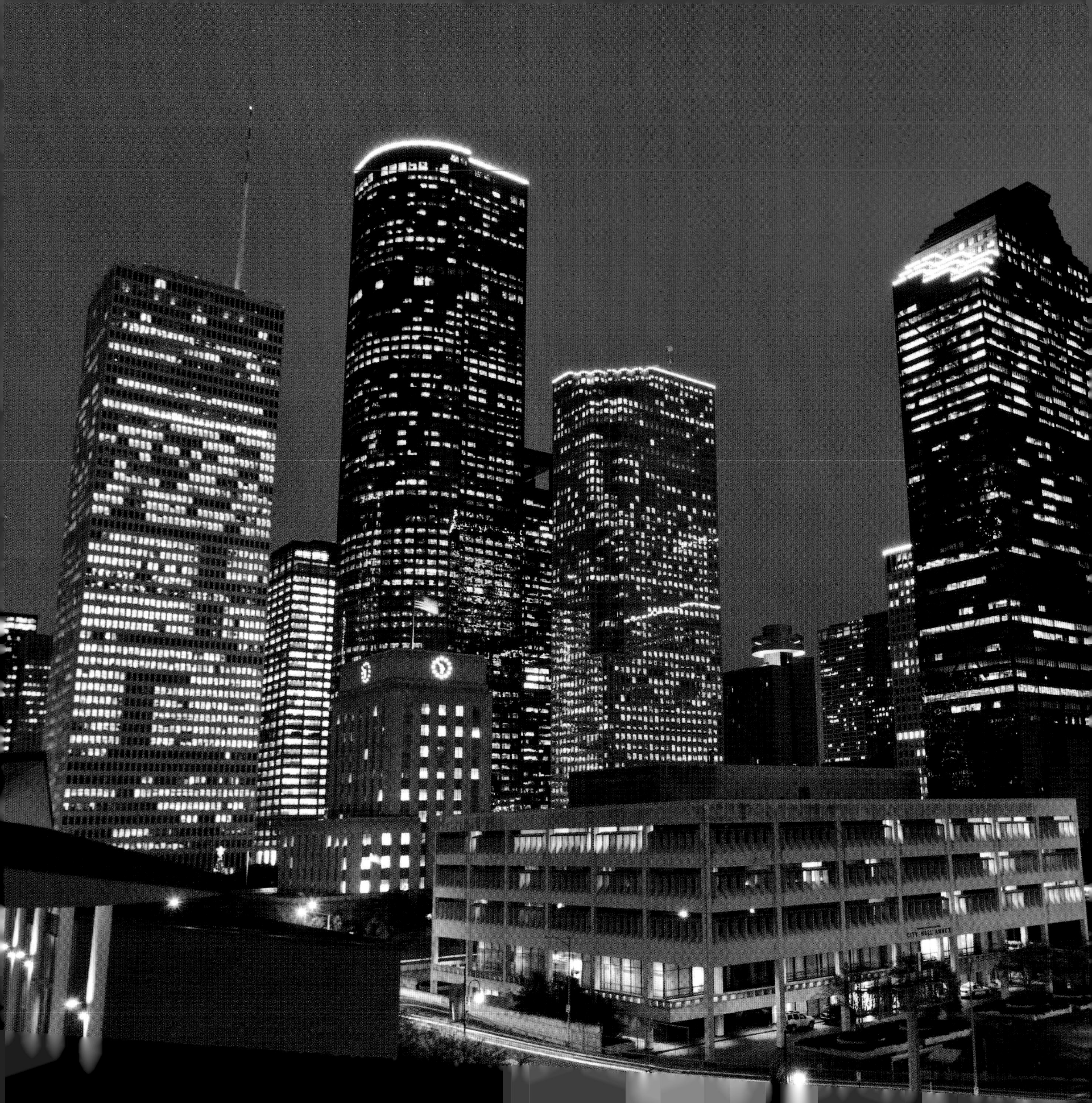
CITY HALL ANNEX

ABOVE: Business and government have made a concerted effort to revitalize downtown Houston in the past several decades. Today, eclectic bars and restaurants dot the Central Business District.

LEFT: The skyline of Houston as seen from near the Pierce Elevated.

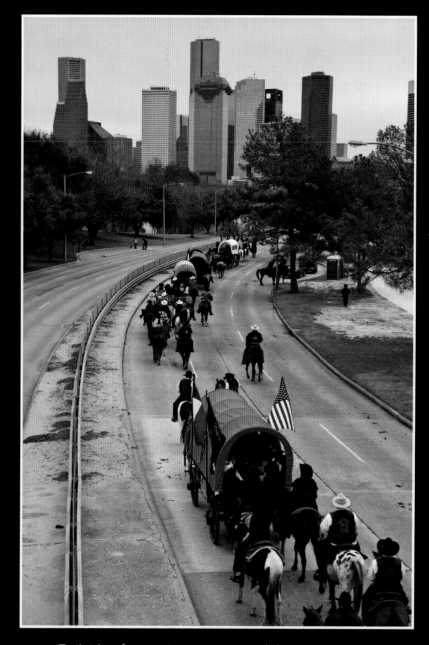

ABOVE: Trail riders from various groups travel down Memorial Drive on their way to the 2012 Houston Livestock Show and Rodeo's parade through downtown Houston.

LEFT: Sunset over the Katy Prairie. The Houston area was once a vast stretch of prairie crisscrossed with bayous and streams. Remnants of the prairie still exist west of town.

FOLLOWING PAGE: The natural flow of Buffalo Bayou has been preserved. Here it meanders along the Allen Parkway west of downtown Houston.